We are all failures—

at least,

all the best of us are.

J.M. BARRIE

Ever tried. Ever failed. No matter.

Try again. Fail again.

FAIL
BETTER.

a book by HERTER STUDIO

RUNNING PRESS
PHILADELPHIA · LONDON

Failure seldom stops you.

What stops you is the fear of failure.

JACK LEMMON

Jimmy Carter, elected president of the United States in 1976, presided over a country crippled by ongoing international crises and the worst economic recession since the Great Depression. He was soundly defeated in the 1980 election by Ronald Reagan after only one term in office. After his presidency, Carter dedicated himself to humanitarian projects, both in the United States and abroad, and in 2002 he was awarded the Nobel Peace Prize.

Never confuse a single defeat with a final defeat.

F. SCOTT FITZGERALD

Walt Disney went bankrupt. Several times.

You may not realize it when it happens,
but a kick in the teeth may be
the best thing in the world for you.

WALT DISNEY

Thomas Edison experimented with over 6,000 materials to use as filament in a light bulb before he found the one that worked.

I have not failed.

I've just found 10,000 ways that won't work.

THOMAS EDISON

In 1901, after failing in their launch of the largest glider ever flown, the Wright brothers predicted that man would probably *not* fly in their lifetime. Nonetheless, they continued to learn from their failed flights, revising and retesting new machines. By 1903, they had designed a 700-pound craft they called "The Flyer." After two failed attempts, one of which resulted in a minor crash, Orville took the Flyer for a 12-second, sustained flight on December 17, 1903. It was the first successful, powered, piloted flight in history.

Only those who dare to fail greatly

can ever achieve greatly.

ROBERT F. KENNEDY

Always do what you are afraid to do.

RALPH WALDO EMERSON

The Edsel was introduced by the Ford Motor Company in 1957. The sales goal for its first production year was 100,000 to 200,000 cars. Falling far short of this, Ford sold merely 100,847 cars over the entire three years of Edsel production. While fewer than 6,000 Edsels survive today, Ford remains the second largest automaker in the world.

Failure is simply the opportunity
to begin again, this time more intelligently.

HENRY FORD

In 1919, Professor Robert Goddard published a scientific paper entitled "A Method for Reaching Extreme Altitudes," which suggested that human space travel was possible. His ideas were ridiculed by the news media, with the *New York Times* claiming that "Professor Goddard . . . does not know the relation of action to reaction . . . he only seems to lack the knowledge ladled out daily in our high schools." As Apollo astronauts headed for the moon in July 1969, the *New York Times* printed an apology for its 1920 editorial against Goddard. Today, he is commonly considered to be the father of modern rocketry.

I cannot give you the formula for success,
but I can give you the formula for failure—
which is: Try to please everybody.

HERBERT B. SWOPE

After Fred Astaire's first screen test in 1933, the memo from the testing director of MGM read, "Can't act. Can't sing. Slightly bald. Can dance a little." Astaire once observed that "The higher up you go, the more mistakes you are allowed. Right at the top, if you make enough of them, it's considered to be your style."

There is no failure. Only feedback.

ROBERT ALLEN

After the success of the show *South Pacific,* composer Oscar Hammerstein put an ad in *Variety* that listed a dozen or so of his failures. At the bottom of the ad, he wrote: "I did it before, and I can do it again."

He who has never failed somewhere,

that man cannot be great.

Failure is the true test of greatness.

And if it be said, that continual success is a proof that a

man wisely knows his powers—

it is only to be added, that, in that case,

he knows them to be small.

HERMAN MELVILLE

No pressure, no diamonds.

MARY CASE

Babe Ruth struck out 1,330 times during twenty-two seasons of play. (He also hit 714 home runs.)

Every strike brings me closer
to the next home run.

BABE RUTH

Winston Churchill failed sixth grade. He was subsequently defeated in every election for public office until he became prime minister at the age of sixty-two. He later wrote, "Never give in, never give in, never, never, never, never—in nothing, great or small, large or petty—never give in except to convictions of honor and good sense. Never, Never, Never, Never give up."

Success is the ability to go from one failure to another
with no loss of enthusiasm.

WINSTON CHURCHILL

In the mid-1980s, Coca-Cola was manufacturing one of the world's most popular, most successful, and most iconic brands. But in an attempt to stave off the encroaching Pepsi, Coke decided to "update" the taste of their cola and launched "New Coke" in April of 1985. New Coke was an unmitigated disaster. Only three months later, executives held a press conference announcing the return of the original formula. "We have heard you," said Roberto Goizueta, then chairman of Coca-Cola.

A fall from the third floor hurts as much
as a fall from the hundredth.
If I have to fall, may it be from a high place.

PAULO COELHO

Vincent van Gogh created over 800 paintings during his lifetime. He sold only one.

Do not fear mistakes, there are none.

MILES DAVIS

The British writer John Creasey received 743 rejection slips before going on to publish 562 books in at least 5,000 different editions in twenty-eight languages. Creasey wrote each of his books out in longhand, revising them five or six times before going to press.

Half the failures of life arise

from pulling one's horse

as he is leaping.

AUGUSTUS HARE

If a thing is worth doing,
it is worth doing badly.

G.K. CHESTERTON

Elvis Presley was fired after just one show at the Grand Ole Opry. Jim Denny, the general manager of the Opry told the young singer, "You ain't going nowhere, son. You ought to go back to driving a truck."

Failure is the condiment
that gives success its flavor.

TRUMAN CAPOTE

Albert Einstein did not speak until he was four years old and didn't read until he was seven. His teacher described him as "mentally slow, unsociable, and adrift forever in his foolish dreams." He was expelled and refused admittance to the Zurich Polytechnic School.

It's not that I'm so smart,
it's just that I stay with problems longer.

ALBERT EINSTEIN

F.W. Woolworth began his life as a farm worker, eventually landing a job at a feed store. It is said that his employers wouldn't allow him to wait on customers because he "didn't have enough sense." He went on to open over 1,000 five-and-dime stores worldwide, and in 1913, the Woolworth Building was erected in New York City (which he famously paid for in cash). At the time, it was the world's largest skyscraper.

There is the greatest practical benefit
in making a few failures early in life.

THOMAS HENRY HUXLEY

In his sophomore year, Michael Jordan failed to make his high school varsity basketball team. He has said, "I was very disappointed, and I thought the coach had made a mistake. But my mother said the best thing for me to do was to prove to the coach that he was wrong. And I started working on my game the day after I was cut."

If I had to select one quality, one personal
characteristic that I regard as being most highly corre-
lated with success, whatever the field,
I would pick the trait of persistence. Determination.
The will to endure to the end,
to get knocked down seventy times and
get up off the floor saying,
"Here comes number seventy-one!"

RICHARD M. DEVOS

You fail in your thoughts
or you prevail in your thoughts only.

HENRY DAVID THOREAU

Alfred Butts invented the game of SCRABBLE after he lost his job as an architect during the Depression. Butts fastidiously studied the front page of the *New York Times* to calculate how often each of the twenty-six letters of the English language was used.

We only think
when we are confronted
with a problem.

JOHN DEWEY

Abraham Lincoln was elected to Congress on his third try. At the end of his term, he failed to be reelected. When he was forty-five, he ran for the Senate and failed to be elected. At forty-seven, he ran for the vice presidency and again lost. Four years later, Lincoln was elected the sixteenth president of the United States.

My great concern is not whether you
have failed, but whether you are
content with your failure.

ABRAHAM LINCOLN

In the 1980s Donald Trump amassed a fortune as a real estate developer and at the end of the decade had an estimated personal net worth of $1.7 billion. But with the decline of the real estate market in the early 1990s, the Trump Organization found itself nearly $900 million in the red and struggling to fight bankruptcy. Trump was also beset by personal scandals around his divorce to Ivana Trump and subsequent marriage to Marla Maples. Trump never quit: he built his business back up again to financial success and in 1997 was reported to be worth close to $2 billion.

Failure?

I never encountered it.

All I ever met were temporary setbacks.

DOTTIE WALTERS

There can be no real freedom
without the freedom to fail.

ERICH FROMM

R. Buckminster Fuller built his geo-
desic domes by starting with a delib-
erately failed dome and making it "a
little stranger and a little stronger . . .
a little piece here and a little piece
there, and suddenly it stood up."

Learning starts with failure;
the first failure
is the beginning of education.

JOHN HERSEY

Charles Goodyear was convinced of the commercial value of rubber—if only he could find a way to keep it from sticking and melting in the heat. He began experimenting with the material while in debtor's prison, and continued to test the material for years, failing many times and eventually driving his family into poverty. The story goes that in 1839 Goodyear was in town showing off his latest gum-and-sulphur formula. As had happened in the past, snickers rose from the watching crowd. It is said that Goodyear became agitated and, while waving his arms in the air, the gum flew from his hand and landed on a sizzling-hot stove. When he went to scrape it off, he found that he had, finally, discovered weatherproof, or vulcanized, rubber.

We learn wisdom from failure
much more than from success.
We often discover what will do
by finding out what will not do;
and probably he who never made a mistake,
never made a discovery.

SAMUEL SMILES

While serving as vice-president, Dan Quayle famously misspelled "potato" during a school spelling bee. Later, Quayle said, "I should have caught the mistake on that spelling bee card, but as Mark Twain once said, 'You should never trust a man who has only one way to spell a word.'" The quote actually came from President Andrew Jackson. "I should have remembered that was Andrew Jackson who said that," Quayle said later, "since he got his nickname 'Stonewall' by vetoing bills passed by Congress." Quayle was wrong again—having confused Andrew Jackson with Confederate General Thomas J. 'Stonewall' Jackson.

Every failure teaches a man something,
to wit, that he will probably
fail again next time.

H.L. MENCKEN

It would not be better
if things happened to men just as they wish.

HERACLITUS

Jack London has written: "I worked away ironing shirts and other things in the laundry, and wrote in all my spare time. I tried to keep on at both, but often fell asleep with the pen in my hand. Then I left the laundry and wrote all the time, and lived and dreamed again. After three months' trial I gave up writing, having decided that I was a failure, and left for the Klondike to prospect for gold." London received hundreds of rejections before his first story was accepted for publication.

There is much to be said for failure.

It is more interesting than success.

MAX BEERBOHM

Orson Welles's first feature film, *Citizen Kane*—which he wrote, directed, and starred in—is widely considered one of the best films ever made. Welles went on to make dozens more movies (of varying success) but became notorious for having difficulties finishing projects. After World War II, he moved away from the United States for more than thirty years. In his later years, Welles earned a living appearing in television commercials for companies such as Paul Masson wines. Welles has said, "I began at the top and have been making my way down ever since."

A life spent making mistakes is not only more honorable but more useful than a life spent doing nothing.

GEORGE BERNARD SHAW

After forty-two rejections, Samuel Beckett published his first novel, *Murphy,* in 1938.

To be an artist is to fail,

as no other dare fail . . .

SAMUEL BECKETT

A real failure does not need an excuse.

It is an end in itself.

GERTRUDE STEIN

The quotes and stories in this book came from many sources, including:
faculty.marymt.edu/learning/famous_flops.htm, www.randomterrain.com, www.museum
marketingtips.com, www.quotationspage.com, www.freedomsnest.com,
www.heartquotes.com, www.greatquotes.com, www.cyber-nation.com, www.quotelady.com,
www.bartelby.com, www.anecdotage.com, www.biography.com, and www.about.com.

. . .

9 8 7 6 5

Library of Congress Control
Number: 2005933406

ISBN 978-0-7624-2514-3

This book may be ordered from the
publisher. Please include $2.50 for
postage and handling. *But try your
bookstore first!*

Running Press Book Publishers
2300 Chestnut Street
Philadelphia, PA 19103-4371

Visit us on the web!
www.runningpress.com

produced in association with:

Herter Studio LLC
432 Elizabeth Street
San Francisco, CA 94114
www.herterstudio.com

Design by Debbie Berne

*The title of this book comes from *Worstward Ho* (1984) by Samuel Beckett: "Ever tried.
Ever failed. No matter. Try again. Fail again. Fail better."